# MARKETING WITH A BOOK

# THE SCIENCE OF
# ATTRACTING HIGH-PAYING CLIENTS
## *for Consultants and Coaches*

# HENRY J. DEVRIES

CEO and Co-Founder, Indie Books International

INDIE BOOKS
INTERNATIONAL

ISBN: 1941870147
ISBN 13: 978-1-941870-14-3
Library of Congress Control Number: 2015902469

Designed by Joni McPherson, mcphersongraphics.com

INDIE BOOKS INTERNATIONAL, LLC
2424 VISTA WAY, SUITE 316
OCEANSIDE, CA 92054

www.indiebooksintl.com

# { DEDICATION }

*This book is dedicated to my greatest mentors:*
*Mark LeBlanc, Dr. David Maister, and Dr. Glen Broom.*
*This book is also dedicated to the Indie Books International*
*team and advisors.*

Ann LeBlanc
Chris Stiehl
Damon Friedman
Dan Janal
David Newman
Denise Montgomery
Devin DeVries
Don Sevrens
Jack DeVries
Jennifer Lentin
John Davern
Joni McPherson
Jordan DeVries
Karla Rosenstein
Ken Hugins
Kiana Moyers
Larry Binderow
Mark LeBlanc
Michael Malone
Michael Podd
Ned Steele
Patty Vogan
Robert Bradford
Scott Ramsey
Vikki DeVries

# { CONTENTS }

# { FOREWORD }

As a professional with expertise, nothing will serve you better as a marketing tool than the independent publishing of your book. You hold in your hands a book that can chart a plan for your book to shine a light on your work, position you as an expert and lead you to more business.

I have run my company, Small Business Success, for more than twenty-three years. I have given more than 1,000 presentations and coached more than 1,000 small business owners on how to grow a business. The majority of these coaching clients and audience members are small practice and working solo professionals.

It is hard to imagine what my career would have looked like, if I had not published my first book, *Growing Your Business*, in late 1999. We have moved more than 50,000 copies of that little book, and have averaged a quantity order of fifty or more every week since it was first published. My second independently-published book, *Never Be the Same*, was inspired by my 500-mile trek across Spain. After *Never Be the Same* was published I inked a six-figure speaking tour with J.P. Morgan Chase Bank.

One thing is for certain: my career would not be where it is today without having published these two books. In *Marketing with a Book* Henry DeVries will lead and guide you on how a book can help define your career and put you on the map.

I met Henry for a cup of coffee one morning in La Jolla, California in the year 2001. He was so taken by my book *Growing Your Business* that he ordered fifty copies and began gifting them to his clients and prospects. Seven years later he reached out to me and invited me to speak at one of his Marketing with a Book Summits. At the time of this printing, we have conducted over forty Marketing with a Book & Speech Summits for professionals on what can happen when you write the right book.

Henry has been involved with over 150 book projects on everything from conception, strategy, ghostwriting, developmental editing to all facets of book marketing, publicity and promotion. He will be the first to tell you that, while marketing books does matter, the real profit is in what can result from publishing your book: selling more services.

Living your dream and doing your life's work will take on new meaning when you use your book to launch or advance your career. Take your time, read carefully and take good notes. Then make the courageous decision to boldly go where few professionals go. Don't cobble together resources for self-publishing your book—assemble the right team to help you write the right book and independently publish your book to traditional book-publishing standards.

Some days you will need a push. Other days we will pull you through when you might get stuck or stalled out. Keep writing. The world needs to read you. And Henry and I are cheering you on!

Mark LeBlanc

Speaker, Coach, Pilgrim and Author of *Growing Your Business* and *Never Be the Same*

President of Small Business Success, Chairman of Indie Books International

# { ACKNOWLEDGMENTS }

This is what Henry likes to think about and thank about. I would like to thank my creator, my parents, my sisters, my children, my mentors, my clients, my students, my colleagues, and my mastermind for all they have given me. My blessings include a positive mental attitude, sound physical health, harmony in human relationships, freedom from fear, hope of future achievement, faith in my creator, a willingness to share abundance with others, a labor of love, an open mind on all subjects, knowledge of how to have self discipline, insights on how to understand people, and financial security through the knowledge of how to create a business that serves the wants of others. In no way am I perfect, but I am shooting for extraordinary. May all who read this have cash flow and time to enjoy it.

GLASBERGEN

"I laughed, I cried, it became a part of me. I must hire the author to be our next IT consultant."

# { CHAPTER 1 }

# The Science of Attracting
# HIGH-PAYING CLIENTS

**M**anagement visionary Peter Drucker said, "There is only one valid definition of business purpose: to create a customer." To do this, an independent consultant or a coach must answer three classic questions: What is my business? Who is my client? What does my client consider valuable? (Drucker, 1954, *The Practice of Management*).

The number one challenge for independent consultants and coaches is creating new clients. Ironically, many consultants and coaches feel marketing is too time consuming, expensive, or undignified. Even if they try a marketing or business development program, most consultants and coaches are frustrated by a lack of results. They even worry if marketing would ever work for them. And no wonder. According to a researcher from the Harvard Business School, the typical sales and marketing hype that works for retailers and manufacturers is not only a waste of time and money for consultants and coaches, it actually makes them less attractive to prospective clients.

However, research has proven there is a better way. There is a proven process for marketing with integrity and getting an up to 400 percent to 2000 percent return on your marketing investment. At our firm, Indie Books International, we call it the Educating Expert Model, and the most successful professional service and consulting firms use it to get more clients than they can handle.

To attract new clients, the best approach for consultants and coaches is to demonstrate expertise by sharing valuable information through writing and speaking. For consultants and coaches, this I believe with my heart of hearts: the number one marketing tool is a book and the number one marketing strategy is a speech. Research shows independent consultants and coaches can fill a pipeline with qualified prospects in as little as thirty days by offering advice to prospects on how to overcome their most pressing problems.

What should consultants and coaches do to increase revenues? First, understand that generating leads is an investment and should be measured like any other investment. Next, quit wasting money on ineffective means like brochures, advertising, and sponsorships. The best marketing investment you can make is to get help creating informative websites, hosting persuasive seminars, booking speaking engagements, and getting published as a newsletter columnist and eventually book author.

Rather than creating a brochure, start by writing how-to articles. Those articles turn into speeches and seminars. Eventually, you gather the articles and publish a book through a strategy called print-on-demand self publishing (we've done it in under ninety days and for less than a $1,000 for clients). Does it work? Here are a list of three business best-seller titles that started out self-published, according to a March 2005 article in *Southwest Airlines Spirit*:

▶ *The One Minute Manager* by Kenneth Blanchard and Spencer Johnson: picked up by William Morrow & Co.

▶ In *Search of Excellence*, by Tom Peters (of McKinsey & Co.): in its first year, sold more than 25,000 copies directly to consumers—then Warner sold 10 million more.

▶ *Leadership Secrets of Attila the Hun*, by Weiss Roberts: sold half a million copies before being picked up by Warner.

Even if you believe in the Educating Expert Model, how do you find time to do it and still get client and administrative work done? No business ever believes they have too much time on their hands. Nothing worth happening in business ever just happens. The answer is to buy out the time for marketing. You need to be involved, but you should not do this all on your own. Trial and error is too expensive of a learning method. Wouldn't it be better if someone helped you who knows the tricks and shortcuts? We can show you how to leverage your time and get others to do most of the work for you, even if you are a solo practitioner.

How much should independent consultants and coaches invest in marketing? That depends on your business goals, but here are some norms. Law firms generally spend about 2 percent of their gross revenues on marketing, and the average expenditure is about $136,000. Marketing costs for accounting firms average about 7 percent to 10 percent of gross revenue, according to a November, 15, 2001 article in *The New York Times*. The typical architecture, engineering, planning, and environmental consulting firm spend 5.3 percent of their net service revenue on marketing, according to ZweigWhite's 2003 Marketing Survey of A/E/P & Environmental Consulting Firms. Mark LeBlanc, author of *Growing Your Business*, has coached more than one thousand consultants and coaches and advises them to invest 35 percent of gross revenues into business development and 15 percent into office and administration expenses.

Does the Educating Expert Model work? In the last fifteen years my training company, the New Client Marketing Institute, and my publishing company, Indie Books International, has had very good results guiding independent consultants and coaches to increased revenues through more new clients, more fee income per client, and more money from past clients. Here are just a few concrete examples:

▶ Through an informational website and electronic newsletter we helped create, one marketing consultant added an additional $100,000 in revenue from speaking engagements and sales of information products within two years.

▶ In forty-five days one client, who is a marketing service provider for the home building industry, was able to launch a website and education expert campaign that helped him double his business in a year.

▶ Using one strategy alone a web marketing business client was able to double his income and add $100,000 of revenue in one year through just one strategy.

▶ By switching over to the model, a marketing services client was able to receive a 2000 percent return on investment from its new marketing campaign that featured how-to advice seminars and articles from senior executives.

▶ When one firm gave up cold calling and switched to our model, the quality of their leads dramatically improved and closed deals quickly increased by 25 percent.

▶ Using these strategies of seminars and getting published, a client has grown in a few years from a regional practice to a national firm.

▶ A well established regional firm reported they were able to accomplish more in six months with our methods than they had in three years on their own.

▶ An advertising agency used the strategy to double revenues from $4.5 to $9.6 million in five years and earn a spot in the Ad Age 500.

Being a published author is the quickest path

to becoming an expert that attracts new clients. So why doesn't every business have a book?

Thanks to new technologies, today it is not only possible to independently publish a professional-looking copy of your book for under $6,000, you can also market the book (traditional version and e-book) through reputable sales channels.

A decade ago, there weren't too many options for consultants and coaches to get into print as a book author. If a traditional publisher wasn't interested in your manuscript, your only other option was to spend tens of thousands of dollars with a vanity press or custom printer. And then, without ready distribution, good luck trying to sell the books.

But that has all changed because alternative indie publishers are able to print both paperback and hardcover books as they're needed due to the bold new digital publishing technology known as "print-on-demand." Going digital allows books to be produced in small quantities — even one at a time — almost instantaneously. No longer does publishing require behemoth offset presses, hangar-size warehouses, and fleets of trucks.

These alternative indie publishers — like my company — have made a conscious decision to offer their services to everyone, rather than give control to an elite clique of editors and agents, as is often true in traditional publishing. The author decides what the public reads, and the public decides if it makes good reading or not. It is a purely market-driven approach, and allows almost anyone to make a new book available to millions of readers, at a small fraction of the cost of traditional publishing methods.

There are challenges, of course. Because print-on-demand books are not typically stocked on bookstore shelves, authors need to do a good job of marketing through publicity, direct mail, and the Internet. But if you are a nonfiction author willing to be a self-promoter and whose book targets an identifiable market, then alternative publishing may be right for you.

Print-on-demand has enormous implications for writers, readers, publishers, and retailers. Because titles are produced "on demand," there are never wasted copies ("remaindered" as they used to be dubbed in the old days). Paperbacks and hardcover books are priced competitively, with authors receiving royalties of 30 percent or more. Compare those with traditional publishing industry standards of 5 to 10 percent, and the appeal becomes a bit clearer still.

What about the writing? If you can write articles, then you can write a book. And if you can't, hire a freelance ghostwriter to help you do it.

EDITORIAL DEPT.

GLASBERGEN

"We'd like you to condense your novel into something that younger people will want to read...in 140 characters or less."

# { CHAPTER 2 }
## Creating a Book
# BLUEPRINT

Before you write a book (or work with a ghostwriter to help you write a book), you need a plan. By following the questions in this chapter a consultant can create a blueprint for a book that will attract clients. The important aspect to focus on is to have the book in alignment with the area of consulting expertise.

My philosophy is that a book should position a consultant, professional, or coach as a subject matter expert. The key to attracting high-paying clients is to be sought out for your expertise on a particular subject.

## The Book Store Question

Visit a bookstore like Barnes and Noble (if, by the time you read this, there are any bookstores left in the world). The average Barnes and Noble bookstore has about 200,000 different books available for sale. Take a moment to study the bookstore and you will quickly see the organization scheme (maybe your book will only be available online, but Amazon.com and BarnesandNoble.com follow the same organizational structure).

The first question to ponder for your book is: where will my non-fiction book be shelved in a Barnes and Noble store? Here are your thirty-nine choices. Choose one and only one.

1. African Americans
2. Antiques & Collectibles
3. Art, Architecture & Photography
4. Bibles & Bible Studies
5. Business
6. Christianity
7. Computer & Technology
8. Cookbooks, Food & Wine
9. Crafts & Hobbies
10. Education & Teaching
11. Engineering
12. Entertainment
13. Foreign Languages
14. Games
15. Gay & Lesbian
16. Health, Diet & Fitness
17. History
18. Home & Garden
19. Humor
20. Judaism & Judaica

21. Law

22. Medicine

23. New Age & Spirituality

24. Parenting & Family

25. Pets

26. Philosophy

27. Politics & Current Events

28. Psychology & Psychotherapy

29. Reference

30. Religion

31. Science & Nature

32. Self Improvement

33. Sex & Relationships

34. Social Sciences

35. Sports & Adventure

36. Study Guides & Test Prep

37. Travel

38. True Crimes

39. Weddings

## Business Subsections

Let's assume, if you are like most consultants and coaches, that your book would be in the business shelves. But where exactly? The business shelves are divided into subsections. Which subsection category would work for you? (You cannot make up a new category, it has to fit into one of these.)

1. Accounting
2. Business & Commercial Law
3. Business Biography
4. Business History
5. Careers & Employment
6. Economics
7. Human Resources
8. International Business
9. Libros en Español
10. Management & Leadership
11. Marketing & Sales
12. Personal Finance & Investing
13. Professional Finance & Investing
14. Real Estate
15. Small Business
16. Women in Business

## Speaking Engagement Topics

One of the most important ways to promote a book, and your consulting practice, is through public speaking. The following are the speech classifications from Vistage International, the largest CEO peer group in the world.

The following is how Vistage categorizes its speakers. Where would your speech fit on the Vistage list? The eight main categories are: Beyond Business, Business Services, General Business, Finance & Accounting, Human Resources, Marketing & Sales, Personal/ Professional Development, and Technology.

### BEYOND BUSINESS

Family & Relationships
Health & Well Being
Leisure/Entertainment
Politics & World Events
Religion & Spirituality
Personal Finances

Purpose & Passion

Mortality & Death

## BUSINESS SERVICES

Environmental Concerns

Facilities Planning/Management

Insurance/Risk Management

Legal Services Patents, Trademarks & Copyrights

Real Estate

Security

Transportation

## FINANCE & ACCOUNTING

Banking/Financing

Bankruptcy

Credit & Collection

Economics

Financial Management

Financial Systems

IPOs

Purchasing/Inventory

Taxes

## GENERAL BUSINESS

Benchmarking

Board of Directors/Advisors

Business Brokerage, Mergers &
Acquisitions

Change

Consultant

Evaluation & Selection

Corporate Communications

Corporate Culture

Creativity/Innovation

Crisis Management/Turnarounds

Ethics

Family Business

Franchising

Future Trends

Government Regulations

Growth Management

Industry Issues

International Business

Joint Ventures/Strategic Alliances

Management

Organizational Development & Lifecycles

Productivity & Process Improvement

Project Management

Strategic Planning & Visioning

Valuation

## HUMAN RESOURCES

Compensation & Benefits

Employee Termination

Employment & Labor Law

Hiring, Recruiting & Retention

Mentoring/Coaching

Motivation/Empowerment

Outsourcing, Alternative Employment

Performance Mgmt. & Appraisal

Program/Policy Design & Compliance

Safety in the Workplace

Teambuilding, Conflict Resolution

Training, Management Development

Unions/Organized Labor

Workers' Compensation

Workforce Diversity

Manufacturing/Distribution

Automation

Distribution

Industrial Engineering

Manufacturing

Plant/Warehouse Management

Product Research and Development

Product Safety

## MARKETING & SALES

Branding

Customer Service

Market Research

Marketing

Pricing

Public Relations/Advertising

Sales & Sales Force Management

## PERSONAL/PROFESSIONAL DEVELOPMENT

Communication/Presentation Skills

Delegation

Goal Setting

Leadership Assessment

Leadership/Role of CEO

Life Planning & Personal Growth

Meeting Planning & Facilitation

Negotiation

Problem Solving/Decision Making

Productivity/Time Management

Retirement/Succession Planning

Stress Management

Women in Business

Self Knowledge

## TECHNOLOGY

Computer Security

Internet, Electronic Commerce

Technology Design/Development

Technology Evaluation/Selection

Technology Strategy and Management

Technology Training & Support

Technology, New & Emerging

Telecommunications

## Pulling it All Together:
# YOUR SUBJECT MATTER EXPERTISE

What subject matter expert positioning do you want? Based on the exercise of where your book will be placed in Barnes and Noble and what topic Vistage CEOs would hear you speak on, complete the following:

This book will position me as a _____ subject matter expert. The book also opens up multiple opportunities for speaking engagements and publicity around the subject of future trends in _____ .

## Preliminary Book Structure

**What will the look and feel of the book be?**
Here are some options:

▶ Textbook (50,000+ words)

▶ Business How-To (35,000 to 45,000 words)

► Tips Book (10,000 to 15,000 words)

► Parable Book (7,000 to 10,000 words)

## What will this book convey?

► New information

► More information

► Better information

► Different information

### How will you publish the book?

► Traditional publisher (you will need a proposal to get an agent and/or publisher, see Appendix B for example)

► Indie publisher with team of experts

► Cobble together a team and self publish

## What Type of Story?

Every business book should tell a story. There are eight great meta stories that humans want to hear over and over again. What type of story are you telling? There are eight basic story structures a book can take, based on the classic eight structures that almost all "stories" follow. This is based on *The Seven Basic Plots: Why We*

*Tell Stories*, a 2004 book by British journalist Christopher Booker, a Jungian-influenced analysis of stories and their psychological meaning. I compared Booker's eight categories and discovered the same rules apply to the greatest business non-fiction books of all time. Here are the eight categories:

1. **MONSTER.** A terrifying, all-powerful, life-threatening monster whom the hero must confront in a fight to the death.  An example of this plot is seen in *Beowulf, Jaws, Jack and the Beanstalk*, and *Dracula*. Most business books follow this plot. There is some monster problem in the workplace, and this is how you attack it. Business book example: *Slay the E-Mail Monster, The E-Myth Revisited, Whale Hunters, Growing Your Business*

2. **UNDERDOG.** Someone who has seemed to the world quite commonplace is shown to have been hiding a second, more exceptional self within. Think *The Ugly Duckling, Cinderella, Jane Eyre, Rudy,*

and *Clark Kent* ("Superman"). The business books in this category discuss how someone raised themselves up from nothing to success, a typical rags-to-riches story. One of Henry's early favorites was *Up From Slavery* by Booker T. Washington. Donald Trump books don't count. He raised himself up from riches to mega riches. Business book examples: *Moneyball*, *Up the Organization*, *Grinding it Out*

3. **QUEST.** From the moment the hero learns of the priceless goal, he sets out on a hazardous journey to reach it. Examples  are seen in *The Odyssey*, *The Count of Monte Cristo*, and *Raiders of the Lost Ark*. Business book examples: *The HP Way*, *In Search of Excellence*, *The One Minute Manager*, *How to Win Friends and Influence People*, *How to Close a Deal Like Warren Buffett*, *Never Be the Same*

4. **ESCAPE.** The hero or heroine and a few companions travel out of the familiar

surroundings into another world completely cut off from the first. While it is at first wonderful, there is a sense of increasing peril. After a dramatic escape, they return to the familiar world where they began. *Alice in Wonderland* and *The Time Machine* are obvious examples, but T*he Wizard of Oz* and *Gone with the Wind* also embody this basic plotline. Business book examples: *The Prodigal Executive*, *The Innovator's Dilemma*

5. **COMEDY.** Think of the movies *Tootsie* and *Some Like it Hot*. Following a general chaos of misunderstanding, the characters

tie themselves and each other into a knot that seems almost unbearable; however, to universal relief, everyone and everything gets sorted out, bringing about the happy ending. This is really about solving a problem with a wacky idea. Shakespeare's comedies come to mind, as do Jane Austen's novels like *Emma*. Business book example:

*2030: What Really Happens to America, A Whack on the Side of the Head, How I Lost My Virginity, Swim with the Sharks*

6. **TRAGEDY.** This is about solving a problem by going against the laws of nature, society, or God. A character through some flaw or lack of self-understanding is increasingly drawn into a fatal course of action which leads inexorably to disaster. *King Lear, Othello, The Godfather, Madame Bovary, The Picture of Dorian Gray, Breaking Bad, Scarface,* and *Bonnie and Clyde*—all flagrantly tragic. Business book example: *Too Big to Fail, Barbarians at the Gate, Liar's Poker*

7. **REBIRTH.** There is a mounting sense of threat as a dark force approaches the hero until it emerges completely, holding the hero in its deadly grip. Only after a time, when it seems that the dark force has triumphed, does the reversal take place. The hero is redeemed, usually through the life-

giving power of love. Many fairy tales take this shape — also, works like *Silas Marner*, *Beauty and the Beast*, *A Christmas Carol*, and *It's a Wonderful Life*. Business book example: *Out of Crisis*, *Seabiscuit*

8. **MYSTERY.** This appeared from the time of Edgar Allan Poe. From *Sherlock*  *Holmes* to *CSI Miami*, the plot that involves solving a riddle has gained immense popularity in the last 150 years. Business book examples: *Good to Great*, *Think and Grow Rich*, *The Secret*, *Cracking the Personality Code*

## What Type of Audience?

Every subject matter expert has a DNA that guides their expertise. What is yours? Here is an exercise to find out. Follow these steps:

▶ What is the name of your business? Is it clear what you do? Is your name a part of the business?

▶ In eleven words or less, who is your target client and what result do you achieve for them?

▶ What are the pains, worries, and frustrations that you help clients deal with?

▶ What is your solution for helping clients? Do you have a model, methodology, or proprietary process?

▶ What is the common misperception that holds many potential clients back from overcoming their pains, worries and, frustrations?

▶ What do your prospect clients need to do in general to solve their problems that you are the expert in? In other words, do you have basic steps that most clients should follow?

▶ In addition to solving their main problem, what other benefits do clients receive from following the course of action that you advocate?

## Working Title of Your Book

Now, and only now, that you have answered the preceding questions are you ready to brainstorm a working title of your book. Working title means the title you start with to guide the project. Often during the writing of the book a better title will materialize. So be it. But you have to start somewhere.

## Marketing Considerations

Remember, books don't promote authors. Authors promote books. When consultants and coaches promote their books, they are really promoting their consulting practices. Here is a quick checklist of twenty-five marketing items to consider. Create the book with the end in mind.

1.  Testimonial blurbs for book back cover from famous people or companies

2.  Foreword for book written by well-known person

3. Website with PDF of table of contents and chapter one of book

4. Blogsite that you post weekly blogs from book

5. Twitter linked to blogsite

6. Facebook linked to blogsite

7. LinkedIn linked to blogsite

8. E-zine (electronic newsletter) with articles from book

9. PR Newswire news releases on tips from book

10. Review copies sent to journalists and bloggers

11. Free speaking engagements (pro bono)

12. Fee speaking engagements (paid)

13. Small-scale seminars that author hosts

14. Teleseminars that author hosts or appears on

15. Conference based around the book

16. Book launch party

17. Flyer for book

18. Postcard for book

19. Business card for book

20. Articles excerpted from book chapters for publications

21. Internet column based on book

22. Print publication column based on your book

23. Sponsorships for personalized copies of books

24. Institutional buyers that will buy books in quantity

25. Bulk book buyers that will buy books in quantity

*Please know this:* the magic is in the mix. In California we say the universe rewards activity. Back in the Midwest, they say God helps those who help themselves. Use the book to shine a spotlight on your work. Start by asking clients about their pains. Gather information on how to solve those worries, frustrations, and concerns. Be the expert who educates people through books, speeches, and publicity on how they compare to their peers and the best ways to overcome their obstacles. The more prospects you inform how to solve their problems in general, the more will hire you for the specifics. In the words of motivational speaker Zig Ziglar: *"You can get whatever you want in life if you just help enough people get what they want."*

"I'm sending you to a seminar to help you
work harder and be more productive."

# { CHAPTER 3 }
# Top Fourteen Ways to
# GENERATE LEADS

Often consultants and coaches tell me they are frustrated with the quality of their marketing materials, they are concerned with their low profile, or they feel pressure because their efforts are not generating enough new client leads. Are any of these issues for you?

Many do not know there is a body of knowledge about what does and does not work in marketing consultants and coaches. A review of the works of David Maister, Robert Bly, Alan Weiss, and other experts reveals a recurring theme of what does and does not work in independent consultant marketing.

Here are the top fourteen tactics that work, but in descending order of effectiveness (I like to save the best for last). You might not need anything after #8.

14. Cold calling by a business development person (never a principal)

13. Video brochures or CDs that give how-to information

12. Printed brochures that give how-to information

11. Sponsorship of cultural/sports events that appeal to targeted clients

10. Advertising in targeted client industry publications

9.  Direct mail

8.  Publicity

7.  Seminars or conference (ballroom scale) you host

6.  Internet game plan of blogs, e-zines, and social media

5. Networking

4. Community and civic involvement, pro bono work

3. How-to articles in client-oriented press

2. Speeches at client industry meetings

1. Small-scale seminars you host

"Yes, we have *Chicken Soup for the Math Teacher's Soul.*
The price is $475 ÷ 23 x .018² – Y³ + 4X ÷ $73.99999 + 2."

# Who Else Wants To Turn Client Pain Into
# MARKETING GAIN?

If you are a consultant, professional, or coach who is a little frustrated about how to attract enough clients, you are not alone. Many independent consultants and coaches struggle with marketing and hope that networking will bring them enough clients. This isn't exactly hoping and wishing for clients, but it is darn close.

There is a better way to get clients. First you probe for pain, then you educate prospects how to solve their pains in general. The more you educate how to solve their pain in general, the more that will hire you for specific services.

Unfortunately, many consultants and coaches who learn this truth find the idea of writing and speaking about client pain too daunting and even mysterious. Most feel this is only for a select few mega-minds like David Ogilvy, Peter Drucker, or Tom Peters, but that is a miscalculated view. You don't need to write three dozen books and have them translated into thirty languages. Just becoming a local guru can work wonders.

Understanding the psychology of clients provides critical evidence of the validity of the "speak up and get published" approach. Consulting and coaching is what economists sometimes call "credence" goods, in that purchasers must place great faith in those who sell the services. How can potential clients trust you if they never hear what you have to say?

The good news is there exists a body of knowledge that some have discovered to grow their consulting businesses. As an example, management consulting firms like McKinsey & Company pioneered the approach beginning in the 1940s and now have it down to a science. Ad agencies like Ogilvy & Mather refined the art. My name for it is the Educating Expert Model for finding clients.

Did you know that psychologists and sociologists have repeatedly found that people are more motivated to avoid pain than to seek pleasure?

Your target market experiences its own unique frustrations and pains. The secret to maximizing your attraction factor is to articulate the worries, frustrations, and concerns that you solve. As the old adage states, "People don't care what you know, until they know that you care." Truly identifying your market's predicament tells them that you understand and empathize with them.

## The Pain-Into-Gain Riddle

*How will clients hire you unless they trust you?*

*How, in turn, will they trust ideas they have not heard?*

*How, in turn, will they hear without someone to speak?*

*How, in turn, will you speak unless you have a solution?*

*How, in turn, will you have a solution unless you understand their pain?*

*How will you understand their pain unless you listen?*

If you are a consultant or coach who struggles with marketing, you are not alone. Many independent consultants and coaches are tired of the rejection, frustration, and mystery of marketing.

There is a better way to attract clients. The secret is to turn their pain into your gain. Start by asking clients about their pains. Then gather information on how to solve those worries, frustrations, and concerns.

Let us ask you this (now be honest): Do you really understand the problems of your prospects and clients? Or do you just think you know? Make no doubt about it, the stakes are high. Wrong marketing messages will cost you potential clients and lead to more struggles and frustration.

So here's how to become a new client magnet. Each group of prospects experiences its own unique frustrations and pains. What's the secret to crafting a marketing message that will maximize your attraction factor? Ask them (or have someone ask for you) about their pains. Start by asking a sample about their ideal business, and then segue into problems. Listen carefully to the exact words they use (you will want to mimic them in your marketing messages).

Chris Stiehl, a marketing research consultant and my co-author on *Pain Killer Marketing*, created this tool. When you interview some current, past, and potential clients about the pains you solve, here are ten questions you should always ask:

1. Describe for me the "ideal" experience with a _____ (your profession or line of consulting). How do most compare to this ideal?

2. Describe for me a recent time that the experience was less than ideal.

3. What are the three most important aspects of doing business with a_____?

4. If I said a _____ was a good value, what would that mean to you?

5.  In what ways does dealing with a
    _____ cost you
    besides money (time, hassle, effort, etc.)?

6.  What is the biggest pain about working
    with a _____?

7.  Would you recommend a _____
    to a friend or colleague? Why, or why not?

8.  How does working with a _____
    help you make money?

9.  What does a _____
    do really well?

10. If you had the opportunity to work with a
    _____ again,
    would you? Why, or why not?

# { CHAPTER 5 }

# How To Be Paid to MARKET

Would you like to add $100,000 or more to your annual income? Read on.

One day I was taking my two teenage sons from our home in San Diego to Disneyland. Along the way I stopped to give a speech to a group of Orange County business owners while the boys munched on a fast food breakfast in the car.

While that speech generated five figures worth of revenue for me as I picked up various paid speeches and consulting work as a result of my talk, the speaking fee was a few hundred dollars. As I came back to the car I tucked my honorarium check (more honor than rarium) in the glove compartment. My older son Jack, fifteen at the time, asked about the check and I told him these business owners actually paid me to market my services to them. "Sweet," said my son, "that is the perfect crime."

# THE FIVE WAYS TO GET PAID TO MARKET

Here are some more examples of this perfect crime, committed by coaching clients I am especially proud of. A marketing research consultant I coached complained that he wasn't getting any consulting business for the past six months from a Fortune 500 client. There are more ways to get paid than straight consulting, I told him. Often companies that don't have money for consultants and coaches have money in their training budgets. So he organized a seminar, held the event near the company's headquarters and sold eleven seats for $600 a piece to that same Fortune 500 client. After the event, several attendees found some budget and he landed about $75,000 in marketing research consulting projects. Later he charged another client $1,500 (he is worth much more) for a ninety-minute talk at a company meeting that will net him consulting contracts in the five figures.

A public relations firm owner I coached was able to double her revenue in a year (I am talking over $100,000 more) just by having different conversations about her pricing with potential clients. Actually, when she raised her rates, it was a signal to the business community that she was in demand and a hot commodity. But alas, how to make even more money. She soon realized there are only so many hours in a week (168, to be precise) and only so much you can charge clients per hour. To increase her revenue she needed to leverage her time. She created some self-published guide books and started offering her expertise through workshops. This leverages her time and she is creating new streams of revenue.

This chapter is not for those who want to calm their nerves as they approach a podium. There will be no words of wisdom about how to conquer those common fears of public speaking (I hear Toastmasters is great for that). This is about professional speaking, not public speaking. This is for consultants and coaches who know that promoting their business with public speaking is the best way to build credibility and keep their pipeline filled with qualified prospects.

Truly, the best proactive lead generation strategy is to regularly demonstrate your expertise by giving informative and entertaining talks in front of targeted groups of potential new clients. The trick is knowing who to contact to get booked as a speaker and developing a topic that will draw the right audience.

Here are five potential perfect crimes, being paid to market your services. These are venues that write checks to consultants and coaches to speak:

1. **Keynotes and breakouts at association and trade group meetings.** A keynote is typically thirty to ninety minutes and usually focuses on a broad topic of interest to all attendees. A breakout session is one of the side sessions at a meeting and last from forty-five to ninety minutes. This is the glamour field of professional speaking. Competition is fierce and the big fees go to celebrities (the group is trading on their star status to attract attendees). I put speaking at Vistage CEO peer groups (formerly TEC) of about a dozen company presidents for half a day at $500 per speech in this category.

2. **Corporate training.** These are typically half-day or full-day seminars and workshops conducted for a private client, usually a corporation, for a group of its employees. This might be the most

lucrative field for speaking because there are many companies that have training budgets. Several clients who make hundreds speaking for Vistage make thousands when they deliver the same presentations to companies. This one-two punch has made several clients an extra $100,000 per year.

3. **Sponsoring your own public seminars.** This is typically a full-day seminar or workshop where registration is open to the public. You market the event and earn a profit (or loss). This business is about getting people into seats. Many times it is a break-even proposition getting the attendees there, and then you make your real money selling information products and consulting services at the back of the room after the event is over. Fees can range from $800 to $1,000 per day per attendee all the way down to my three-hour Lunch and Learn seminars for $25.

4. **Teaching at colleges and for public seminar companies.** An alternative to

running the seminar yourself is to find a sponsor. This might be for a company like Career Tracks or The Learning Annex. Or you might approach the adult education marketplace through a college or university extended studies program. Typically you might earn 25 percent of what the students pay all the way up to $1,000 for a day.

5. **Speaking at fundraising workshops where you split the gate.** Another alternative to running the seminar yourself is to approach a trade group or association and offer to stage a fundraising seminar. They promote the event to their constituents and you agree to split the profits (typically 50/50 and you may or may not offer them 10 percent of any informational products like books and CDs that you sell in the back of the room after the event).

# THE BEST BOOK ON THE SUBJECT

If you want to read one book on the subject, I recommend *Money Talks: How To Make A Million As A Speaker* by Alan Weiss, author of *Million Dollar Consulting*. If you are really interested in the subject, I personally recommend the Odd Couple CD set Weiss or Patricia Fripp sell on their websites. If you want to join the ranks of the top paid consultants and coaches, those who make $1 million a year, this is a great investment.

Best-selling author Weiss used to give speeches for free. Now his income from professional speaking and consulting totals more than $1 million a year.

Weiss is a contrarian. Many books on professional speaking say you start by coming up with a few great topics. Weiss couldn't disagree more.

"Listen carefully because few in speaking heed the following, and I'm as sure of this advice as any I've offered in seven books: Always define yourself in terms of lasting value to the client," writes Weiss. "When someone asks you, 'What do you speak about?" it's an amateurish question. But when you dignify it and satisfy it with 'I speak about x, y and z,' that's a career-limiting response."

Before studying what Weiss had to say I would say things like "I speak on marketing, I convey networking skills, I provide publicity advice," and so on. That's putting it in speaker's terms. Now I speak in buyer's terms. My speeches improve lead generation, maximize revenues, reduce wasted marketing that erodes profitability, increase lead conversion rates, and challenge attendees to exceed to higher goals. That's what speech buyers, the people who actually write the checks, want to have happen.

What is the value that you bring to the buyers of speeches? Not the participants, but the people who write the checks. This is the star that should guide you as you navigate your paid speaking journey. Speaking clients want their situation improved because of your speech.

"If you don't leave the client in a better position than the client was in before you got there," writes Weiss, "then there is no point in having you there at all."

"This book is defective. I tap the
page and nothing happens!"

# { CHAPTER 6 }
# Thirty Tips to Find Clients Through PUBLIC SPEAKING

This chapter is an example of a numbered tips article. Easy to write and easy to read.

1. First, let's acknowledge a universal truth: Nobody likes public speaking. At least, not at first. A book is the number one marketing tool and a speech is the number one marketing strategy. However, standing in front of a group of strangers can be nerve-wracking. Luckily, there's a cure, and it's simple: practice, practice, practice.

2. Few things make as much client seduction sense as speaking. Your prospects get to

see you and hear you sharing expertise without any risk. Speeches are a perfect opportunity to be seen, heard, and most important, *remembered*.

3. Securing speaking engagements, however, is not as easy as throwing your name into a hat. You have to prove yourself and your credentials: A strong business track record, a unique message worth hearing, and compelling speaking skills.

4. If you need to learn how to speak, join Toastmasters. Not only is such a group likely to attract other success-oriented professionals, it's also a great, low-threat way to pick up practical pointers, watch other dynamic speakers in action, and begin to get used to the idea of speaking to groups.

5. Start with family, friends, and colleagues. Just ask. As with other things in life, our circle of influence is often more connected to what you want than you might realize. Want to talk to local hiring managers at technology firms? Ask around and you

might be surprised how many people in your network can suggest groups you might approach.

6. Package yourself. Write a one-page letter that explains who you are, what your background is, and three to five topics on which you are prepared to speak. Make this your standard "speech pitch." Also make sure you have a one-paragraph biography, introductory paragraphs for each speech, and a pre-written introduction (to you) available for the people who book you.

7. Prepare a thirty-second commercial for your speaking. Condense what you have to offer to an audience as much as possible: "I'm Joann Blough, and I'm an expert on tax savings. I speak to more than twenty groups a year on unique tax strategies, leveraging international tax law, and expanding tax savings through an international approach." Use this "elevator speech" when you network and socialize.

8. Search the Internet for directories of

clubs and organizations. This kind of directory can be an invaluable resource when you're sending out e-mails offering your speaking services.

9. Contact group staff and committee members, who can tell you about each group's procedures for selecting speakers.

10. Contact university continuing education instructors in your field and offer to be a guest lecturer. Be sure to use handouts that are printed on your stationery that includes your phone number and web address. Extended studies students are often more motivated, better educated, and more attuned to forming alliances than the average person in the industry.

11. Or, get paid to speak—as a university extension instructor, or with such organizations as The Learning Annex.

12. Offer to do in-house training for corporations. It's a low-pressure way to hone your skills and really dig deeply

into your subject of expertise. You'll also discover the need to make your speaking more interesting and animated when you're working with a group for a longer period of time—good lessons for anybody who wants to spend more time at the podium.

13. Approach conferences that are scheduled to take place in your area, or in your industry. Send them your speaker's introduction kit and topic list. Follow up with a phone call.

14. After a speech, offer to hold a small roundtable discussion for those who are interested. This can be later in the day — at a coffee break or over cocktails — and is a great way to solidify your position as a trustworthy expert, and to extend the impact and influence of what you've said to the larger group.

15. Consider going pro. The National Speakers Association (NSA) offers practice and networking for experts who get paid to speak. Once you're proficient at talking about your expertise, check them out and watch the opportunities expand.

16. When trying to woo and win clients, consultants and coaches need to remember that nobody loves a salesman. Just ask Scott Love. "The problem with actively selling your professional services to prospective clients is that it screams, 'I have no business right now,'" says Love, an author and an internationally recognized expert on leadership. "And if you have no business, how good can you be?"

17. Love maintains that prospects only want to do business with the sought-after and busy consultants and coaches, not the ones scrambling for new projects. How good can an empty restaurant be if no one is eating there? How good can a professional be if he has to actively solicit business?

18. "Instead of selling, focus on bringing the business to you by creating the perception that you are the premier expert in your field," says Love. "By following four practical steps your credibility factor will skyrocket."

19. The most effective way to build credibility is to create a perception that you are the "guru" in your field. Here are Love's four steps to accomplish that:

20. Step one: Target the industries in which you work. Clearly identify those industries in which your value is the highest.

21. Step two: Contact the associations that serve those industries. Initially speak to

the editor of the association newsletter and offer articles that they can print for free on a subject in which you are an expert, something that solves a problem of their members or helps them raise the bar.

22. Step three: The association editors will never turn you down because they are always looking for good content. In fact, put several articles on your website as a collection for them to download at will. (For an example of how Love set this up, visit his website at www.scottlove.com.)

Tell them that the articles are already written and they don't have to worry about deadlines because the work is done. Ask them to send you a copy of the publication and that they must print your non-salesy byline at the end of the article. "And don't make the byline a commercial," adds Love. "Have just your name, company name, what you do, and your website or e-mail or phone number."

23. Step four: Once your article is printed in their magazine or newsletter, contact the head of their education department or their meeting planner for their conventions. Tell them that you are an expert in your field and are recognized by many of their association members. In fact, tell them to turn to page thirty-seven of this month's magazine so that they can see your article in it. Because you are in their very own publication, they will see you as an expert in their industry. Offer your services in terms of speaking and training for their association.

24. "Charge for this. Don't give it away," says Love. "If you don't charge for your speaking they will believe that you do not value your time or your message. Sure, they know you'll get business from it. But you need to charge for it." Love believes your initial refusal to give it away sends a message that you believe your message has tremendous value.

25. If it ends up that there is no way at all they will pay you, then negotiate something which costs them nothing, but has value to you. Ideas for free remuneration include: getting their mailing list, being a regular columnist in their newsletter, getting free advertising in their newsletter or a banner link on their site to yours, obtaining free advertising in the conference program guide, receiving free sponsorship of an event, and having a free booth at their convention.

26. Whenever you can, charge money for your information. When people see that you value your time and your professional expertise, it sends a signal to the association, which is then conveyed to the rest of the industry.

27. "When you give your presentation, never ever sell your services from the platform," says Love. People hate that and will go out of their way for the rest of their lives to never do business with you if they perceive your breakout session to be a ninety-minute commercial. Instead, give away all of your secrets and tell your audience that anytime they have a quick question that they can call you for no charge. (Be sure to put your phone number and website address at the bottom of every single page of your handouts). The ones that call you are the ones you want to talk to anyway, because they see you as the expert.

28. "And when they call, give them your best advice, letting them know in advance that you cannot spend more than just a few minutes off the clock with them," says Love. "They will then see the value of your expertise, and they will inevitably ask for more information on your services if they see a benefit."

29. "Follow these steps and watch your business explode," concludes Love. "By creating credibility in your firm, you will have a hard time keeping up with all the business that will soon seek you out."

30. Even though surveys consistently show that people would rather visit their in-laws than speak in front of a group, speeches and presentations are absolutely essential to long-term success for consultants and coaches who follow the Educating Expert Model.

# { CHAPTER 7 }

# Cracking Your Marketing
# GENETIC CODE

I s your marketing for clients pathetic or genetic? Pathetic marketing communicates the message that "I'm in business too."

Here is the *Reader's Digest* version on cracking your marketing genetic code. Before you can begin attracting clients, you need to create a marketing genetic code that is attractive to clients. All of your marketing messages, from networking discussions to speeches, will contain the elements of this marketing DNA that positions you as the Educating Expert. Here are ten steps that will help you create these all-important marketing genes.

1. **Name your biz without your name.**
   Create a business name or a website name
   that gives potential clients a hint at the
   results you can produce for them. The
   worst possible business name or website
   name is your name. I know, I know, Ford,
   McKinsey and Price Waterhouse are
   named after the founders. But you are not
   them. At least, not yet. Sorry to say, clients
   don't want us — they want results.

2. **Boil it down.** Write a headline for your
   website and marketing materials that
   describes your audience and the results
   you produce for them. Do this in no more
   than ten words.

3. **Name your client's pain.** What are your
   client's worries, frustrations, and concerns
   that you help solve? This is also called the
   *FUD factor*: fear, uncertainty, and doubt.

4. **How to fix it.** Describe your solution or
   methodology for solving these pains. What
   process do you follow to produce results?
   Offering a proprietary problem-solving

process that you name and trademark is best. This answers the all-important question in their minds: "Why should I do business with you instead of one of your competitors?"

5. **The myths.** State the common misperception that holds many back from getting results. Why doesn't everybody do what you named in step four?

6. **Step by step.** Tell your clients what they need to do in general to solve their problem. Pretend they weren't hiring you and you had to describe the steps they should take for success.

7. **The extras.** List any other benefits they get from following your methods. What other good things do people get when they do what you advise?

8. **Track record.** Elaborate on your track record of providing measurable results for clients. Be specific as much as possible. Use numbers, percentages, and time factors.

9. **Give it away.** Create a website with free tips articles on how to solve these pains. Each article should be about 300 to 600 words. What's a good format? Consider the numbered tips approach you are reading right now (easy to write, easy to read).

10. **An offer they can't refuse.** Make prospects an offer of a free special report on your website. You are offering to trade them a valuable piece of information for their e-mail address. Tell them they will also receive a tips e-newsletter from you. Assure them you will maintain their privacy and they can easily opt off your list any time they want.

## { CHAPTER 8 }

# How To Turn Seminars Into
# INCREASED REVENUE

What do April, March, and October have in common? These are the top three months for consultants and coaches to host a seminar.

To make seminars fill your pipeline with qualified leads, first scrutinize your proposed topic by asking yourself some hard questions. If prospective clients attend this teleseminar, what beneficial information will they receive? Is this information that my competition either cannot, or does not, offer? Is this information a strong enough pull to justify them spending their precious time with us?

Next, examine how you spread the word. Do you have the right e-mail list for prospects (they gave you permission to e-mail them) and mailing list for suspects (these are strangers you don't know yet)? Maybe e-mail and direct mail alone are not enough to deliver enough prospects to your next seminar. A key to attracting high-level executives is to reinforce e-mail direct mail messages with phone calls. These calls also can provide valuable feedback on how prospects view the seminar topic and subject matter.

Event letters or invitations should be mailed or e-mailed approximately four weeks prior to the event. Another e-mail blast a few days before an event can also work well. Give registrants the option to call the 800 number, fax, e-mail or utilize the online event registration application on the Internet to register for an event. When possible, it is helpful to provide an overview of what will be covered.

Here are some business-to-business seminar scheduling guidelines:

▶ No business/corporate seminars on weekends

▶ Independent consultants, professionals, and coaches like weekend seminars

▶ Avoid Monday and Friday for business/corporate seminars

▶ Avoid seminars in a holiday week (Fourth of July, June commencement)

▶ Check for conflicting industry events

> **The best months to hold a seminar, in rank order, are:**
> 1. March
> 2. October
> 3. April
> 4. September
> 5. November
> 6. January
> 7. February
> 8. June
> 9. May
> 10. July
> 11. August
> 12. December

Telemarketing calls can increase registrations 5 percent beyond the registration rate from direct mail. Calling is conducted one to three weeks prior to the event. Many seminar experts recommend three call attempts per contact with voice messages on the first and third attempts.

Typically, only 40 to 50 percent of those who say they will attend a free seminar actually attend. To minimize no-shows, confirmation e-mails and phone calls are two options that boost attendance. Send an e-mail confirmation forty-eight hours prior to the event. The e-mail confirmation will act as a reminder of the event and provide them date, time, location, and directions. E-mail confirmations can greatly increase the attendance rate at the event. But even better is to give the registrant a call forty-eight hours before the event. The personal touch makes an impact.

"Yes, we have *Chicken Soup For The Investor's Soul.*
Do you want to pay cash or buy it on margin?"

# CHAPTER 9

# Five Ways To Increase Your
# PERSUASION POWER

To help prospective clients choose you, give them a persuasive mental shortcut. You can gain trust with clients through a proven persuasive secret called social proof.

With more than one quarter of a million copies sold worldwide, *Influence: The Psychology of Persuasion* by Robert B. Cialdini, PhD has established itself as the most important book on persuasion ever published. In this book, which I highly recommend, Professor Cialdini explains why some people are remarkably persuasive.

The book explains six psychological secrets behind our powerful impulse to comply and how to skillfully use these tactics. The book is organized around these six principles of consistency, reciprocation, authority, liking, scarcity, and social proof.

The principle of social proof states that one shortcut people use to determine what is correct is to find out what other people think is correct. As a rule, we will make fewer mistakes by acting in accord with social evidence than contrary to it. This is why television sitcoms have canned laughter tracks and commercials use man-in-the street testimonial interviews. Or why people want restaurant reviews from websites like Yelp or hotel reviews from websites like TripAdvisor.

The reason social proof is so persuasive is because people are all so information overloaded. Professor Cialdini says his research evidence suggests that the ever-accelerating pace and informational crush of modern life will make automated decision making more and more prevalent.

"You and I exist in an extraordinarily complicated stimulus environment, easily the most rapidly moving and complex that has ever existed on this planet," writes Professor Cialdini. "To deal with it, we need shortcuts. We can't be expected to recognize and analyze all the aspects in each person, event, and situation we encounter in even one day. We haven't the time energy or capacity for it."

How should pain-into-gain consultants and coaches use social proof? The answer is testimonials with measurable results, and here are five ways to do it:

1. **Interview past clients to obtain testimonial quotes you can use.** Sometimes it is best to get an outside

expert like a public relations professional or freelance writer to help you with this. You want to drill down to get measurable results. These include raw numbers (increased sales by $100,000), percentages (improved retention rates to 70 percent, which is triple the industry average) or time (accomplished more in six months than in previous three years).

2. **May I please?** Get permission to use the person's whole name, title, and company name. Just saying "Sally from Kalamazoo" or "Bob from Cucamonga" just doesn't build trust.

3.  **If you don't ask, you don't get.** Ask for testimonial letters on client letterhead that you can reprint and use in proposal packages being given to clients. The more you have to choose from the better.

4.  **Tell me a story.** Ask clients who are willing to be your advocate to record their testimonial stories. One way to do this easily is to hop on a free telephone bridge or use a smartphone app. This can than be used as an audio file on your website or turned into a low-cost audio CD that you can give potential clients.

5.  **Be a name dropper.** Pepper your speeches, seminars, and presentations with accounts of individuals who have benefited from your service. Always make the person seem likable, describe the problem in brief, and give a measurable result you helped achieve. One of my clients said he helped grow businesses. This became so much stronger when he was able to say he helped grow business by as much as 500 percent.

"If a tree falls in the forest, but you don't
hear about it on Facebook, MySpace,
YouTube or Twitter, did it really happen?"

# { CHAPTER 10 }
# Formalize Your
# PROPRIETARY PROCESS

Every book from a consultant or coach should contain their proprietary process for solving client problems. You gain enormous leverage when you formalize something you've probably already got: a proprietary problem-solving process that you will now name and protect by obtaining a trademark.

Your process should have an enigmatic name that prompts questions; you want to be asked to explain it. A proprietary process is not only a marketing asset that will allow you to charge more, but also will make your work less accidental and improve the quality of your service.

# HOW TO WIN CLIENTS WITH A PROPRIETARY PROCESS

When potential clients tell you their problems, they expect you to tell them how you can solve them. This is the moment of truth: The time you explain how you solve problems like theirs. After you suggest a solution, you want them thinking, "At last...someone who understands my problem and really knows what they are doing."

There's an old marketing saying that goes like this: "If you don't have anything unique to advertise about your business, then you should advertise your business for sale." To woo and win clients, you need a distinct problem-solving methodology for your professional service firm, coaching, or consulting company. This is your proprietary process, an approach unique to your firm.

If you go to the Google search engine and type in "proprietary process," you will discover over 550,000 entries as of this writing. Obviously, the proprietary process, as a marketing technique, is gaining currency in the marketplace.

Nashville-based business consultant David Baker says one of the most common mistakes a consulting firm can make is not having a defined, proprietary process. Writing in his newsletter Persuading (available through his website, www.recourses.com), Baker highlights several reasons why a proprietary process is important.

"Process is differentiating, highlighting the uniqueness of your firm with a process that you own," says Baker. Other advantages he cites are that a process demonstrates your experience, makes your work less accidental, and will even allow you to charge more. "Clients are always willing to pay more for packages than individual hours within a fee structure."

A good proprietary process, however, is never a cut-and-dried industry standard lifted from a textbook. Instead, it codifies a firm's particular method of problem-solving, typically identifying and sequencing multiple steps that often take place in the same, defined order. Furthermore, the completed process should have an intriguing name — one that you can trademark.

What are some of these intriguing proprietary process names? Here are a few to ponder:

▶ The I-Innovation Process

▶ The SupporTrak RACE System

▶ The NetRaker Methodology

▶ The Systematic Determination Process

▶ The Persuasion Iteration Process

▶ The Innovation Continuum Methodology

Don't worry if you don't understand what any of these processes do just by hearing the names: That's actually the point. A name that is unique enough to actually qualify to be trademarked will also create the opportunity to explain the process to potential clients.

Don't go overboard, however, and create a name that is all marketing hype with no real service substance. Sometimes a line from a movie says it all. Remember when every burger joint had a secret sauce? In the film *Fast Times at Ridgemont High*, teenage workers from various fast food restaurants reveal what goes into the "secret sauce" for their hamburgers. One says "ketchup and mayonnaise," and the other says "thousand island dressing."

Make sure that some real problem-solving ingredients have gone into the secret sauce of your firm — your proprietary process — and that the name actually reflects your unique approach.

# STEPS TO IDENTIFY YOUR UNIQUE SYSTEM

Most clients are attracted by specialization first, and then by a proprietary process. Here are some recommendations to create your own defined problem-solving system that will help you attract clients.

1.  Outline what you already do to solve client problems.

2.  Break this process down into a series of defined steps (usually from five to seven are enough).

3.  Give the process an intriguing name, typically no more than four words. Begin with "The" and ending with "System," "Process," or "Methodology."

4.  Search the U.S. Patent Office website (www.uspto.gov) to find out whether you can trademark the name (steer clear if it's already been used in your industry).

5.  Seek legal protection of the process as intellectual property through the U.S. Patent Office.

6.  Include the process on your website, but only give enough detail to describe it in general, so you have room to adapt it for each selling situation.

7.  Continually improve the process, and be sure to document the improvements.

# CREATE AN INTERNAL BLUEPRINT

In addition to the process documentation you show your clients, you should have a detailed internal document on how you use the proprietary process. The truism about service businesses is that people come and go, but the process is forever.

According to Professor Christopher Lovelock of the Yale Business School, you should create a blueprint of your business's process, a visual map of the sequence of activities required to complete the process for clients. To develop a blueprint, you need first to identify all of the key activities in the service design and production.

Service blueprints clarify the interactions between clients and members of the firm. "This can be beneficial, since operationally oriented businesses are sometimes so focused on managing backstage activities that they neglect to consider the customer's view of front-stage activities," writes Lovelock in his book *Services Marketing*. "Accounting firms, for instance, often have elaborately documented procedures and standards for how to conduct an audit properly, but may lack clear standards for when and how to host a client meeting or how to answer the telephone when clients call."

# HOW TO TRADEMARK YOUR PROPRIETARY PROCESS

Does what you sell to clients cost more than $1,000? To woo and win clients, you need a distinct problem-solving methodology for your professional service firm, consulting practice, or technology-based service company. This is your proprietary process, an approach unique to your firm.

Are you safeguarding your intellectual assets? Protecting physical property — such as buildings and cars — is an obvious choice for most business people because these things are visible and tangible. We can all see it, stand on it, or ride in it. But what about trade secrets, trade names, and copyrights? Intellectual property is another matter, because it is not easy to see and much harder to value.

Annually the United States issues 100,000 patents, 60,000 trademarks, and more than 600,000 copyrights. The system is beautiful to behold when it goes right.

"As an attorney who has helped protect thousands of products and services in the past decade, I also have seen the unfortunate consequences when things go wrong," says attorney Larry Binderow, a specialist in trademarks, copyright protection, and domestic/international licensing and franchising. "The stakes are high because counterfeit and fraudulent use of intellectual property costs U.S. businesses more than $60 billion per year."

When a mark is registered by the United States Patent and Trademark Office, Bindreow recommends that notice of the registration be given by placing the familiar "circle-R" ® symbol adjacent the mark as used on labels or packaging, and in advertising or similar publications.

According to Binderow, it pays to know the proper use of this symbol (or an alternative form of registration notice) with federally registered trademarks, service marks, collective marks, and certification marks.

# REASONS FOR USING A REGISTRATION NOTICE

Display of a registration notice is not mandatory. Use of the notice is recommended, however, for the following reasons:

1. The notice advises the public of your claim to exclusive use of the mark on goods or services specified in the registration.

2. The notice advises the public that the word or symbol is being used to designate the goods or services of the registration owner, and not merely as an ordinary adjective or product name. The notice also serves as a helpful warning to newspaper or magazine writers to avoid using the mark as a generic term.

3. Should an infringement occur, failure to use a registration notice will limit recovery of damages or profits to the period when the infringer was aware of the existence of the registration.

## ACCEPTABLE FORMS OF REGISTRATION NOTICES

The federal trademark laws specify the following three styles of acceptable notices:

1. ®

2. Reg. U.S. Pat. & TM Off.

3. Registered in U.S. Patent and Trademark Office

"I recommend use of the ® symbol because it is short and easy to insert without upsetting the graphic balance of labels, brochures, and other displays of the registered mark," says Bindreow. "Positioning of the notice is not critical, but the ® symbol is normally used as a superscript immediately after the mark. There is no required minimum size for the ® symbol, and a small, unobtrusive size is perfectly acceptable as long as it is legible."

## POINTS TO CHECK BEFORE USING A REGISTRATION NOTICE

Binderow warns that it is improper to use any of the above-listed registration notices with a mark until a federal registration of the mark has been issued. Mere filing of an application for registration does not authorize use of the notice. Similarly, issuance of a state registration does not authorize use of the ® symbol or the other notice forms listed above. In the interim, a permissible and recommended procedure is to use a™ on trademarks not protected by a federal registration.

"Knock it off, Hon — I'm trying to read!"

# { CHAPTER 11 }

# The Stairway to Heaven:
# HOW TO USE A MENU APPROACH

You wouldn't eat at a restaurant that only offered one meal. You wouldn't enroll your children in a college that offers only one major. You wouldn't subscribe to a cable service that has only one channel. Your clients are no different. They want choices and options.

Give clients a range of choices of how to engage with you. What is the cheapest way to engage with you? Probably a blog and website articles. That is at the bottom of your ladder. What is the ultimate result clients want? What if they wanted all you had to give? That heavenly result should be at the bottom of your stairway.

Here is my stairway. I give you this template so you can come up with your own. The higher the stair step, the bigger the investment in time and money. I am totally fine with wherever a prospect wants to start on the staircase and how high they want to go.

Outsourced VP of Publishing
_____

Book Publisher
_____

Book Ghostwriter
_____

Book Developmental Editor
_____

Book Blueprint
_____

Book Strategy Session
_____

Attend Book and Speech Summit
_____

Buy my Workbook
_____

Buy my Book
_____

Attend my Speech
_____

Read my Blogs and Articles
_____

# THE MENU AND GOLDILOCKS PRICING

No doubt you offer more than one kind of service or level of service; package these creatively in ways that will let clients feel in control of their buying. We use the terms "Silver," "Gold," and "Platinum" as shorthand; you can name your packages whatever you like, so long as it makes sense and implies a scale of value.

"Silver" packages are the lowest level of service you'll offer — bare-bones, no frills, pragmatic, and no-nonsense.

"Gold" packages add more features, frequency, or services; they're the ones most clients will choose, because most people believe moderation is a good thing.

Finally, there's your "Platinum" package. This is the package that will attract the kind of client who shops exclusively at Nordstrom and Neiman-Marcus. This package is for the client who likes to say, "I'm worth it." You may not sell a large number of them, but when you do, you'll be satisfied that you didn't leave money on the table.

Finally, it's important that, regardless of which package your new client chooses, it's still guaranteed. If you can't offer a 100 percent satisfaction guarantee on Silver Package work, consider whether it's worth offering at all. Your reputation is at stake with every client at every level; if you can't afford to do your best work at your lowest

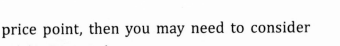

price point, then you may need to consider raising your prices.

## AN EXAMPLE

Company X, below, offers custom publicity widgetry. They offer clients three levels of service.

Which would you choose?

### Platinum:
Bells, whistles, and a tickertape parade

### Gold:
Bells and whistles

### Silver:
Just whistles

Most people, faced with such a choice, tend to purchase the middle option. "Bells and whistles are fine, and we don't need a tickertape parade," goes the typical thinking.

So, load your Platinum package up to the hilt, and rest assured that most potential clients are like Goldilocks. They don't want too much, or too little. They want to buy "just right."

"My master taught me how to speak when I was just a pup. But I didn't get really good at it until I joined Toastmasters."

# CHAPTER 12
# Persuade With a
# STORY

I n closing, the most important element to
include in a book or a speech that attracts
clients are stories. But not just any type of
story.

Consultants and coaches need to share stories
in which they are not the hero. The client needs
to be the hero of the story. There needs to be a
villain problem that is holding the client back.
Finally, you need to be the wise mentor of the
story that helps the client hero overcome the
villain problem.

As my buddy Michael Hague, a screenwriting
teacher and consultant to Hollywood
filmmakers like Will Smith, says: "The story

must be true, but it does not have to be factual." In other words, some literary license is allowed to condense the story down to its essence.

There is only one story you get to tell where you are the hero. I will share that with you last.

# WHY PERSUADE WITH A STORY

In September of 2008 *Scientific American* published an article on "The Secrets of Storytelling: Why We Love a Good Yarn". Please read the entire article, but here is a summary.

According to Jeremy Hsu in *Scientific American*, storytelling is a human universal, and common themes appear in tales throughout history and all over the world (I refer you back to the eight great meta stories in Chapter 2). The greatest stories—those retold through generations and translated into other languages—do more than simply present a believable picture. These tales captivate their audience, whose emotions can be inextricably tied to those of the story's characters.

By studying narrative's power to influence beliefs, researchers are discovering how we analyze information and accept new ideas. A 2007 study by marketing researcher Jennifer Edson Escalas of Vanderbilt University found that a test audience responded more positively to advertisements in narrative form as compared with straightforward ads that encouraged viewers to think about the arguments for a product. Similarly, Melanie Green of the University of North Carolina co-authored a 2006 study that showed that labeling information as "fact" increased critical analysis, whereas labeling information as "fiction" had the opposite effect. Studies such as these suggest people accept ideas more readily when their minds are in story mode as opposed to when they are in an analytical mind-set.

# THREE MUST-HAVE CHARACTERS

This formula is very basic.

Every story needs a hero, a villain, and a mentor. If you are familiar with *The Wizard of Oz*, this would be Dorothy Gale of Kansas, the Wicked Witch of the West, and Glinda the Good Witch of the North. If the first Star Wars movies are more your cup of tea, then we are talking about Luke Skywalker, Darth Vader, and Jedi Knight Master Yoda.

Your client must be the hero of all your stories (save one). Start your story by introducing us to the hero. Make the hero likable. Make us want to root for the hero.

Next introduce us to the problem. In one of my stories I label a bad economy as "the wolf at the door." If you can use a person that represents the issue, so much the better.

Finally, you should be the mentor or wise wizard character of the story. With your advice your hero/client overcomes the villain problem.

Your book and speeches should be peppered with such stories. These stories provide the psychological clues as to why prospects should hire you. There is only one story you tell, and never at the beginning, where you get to be the hero. This is "Your Story," which helps prospects understand why they should engage with you. I close this book with my story.

# MY STORY

Once upon a time my business coach, Gary Hawk, asked me four questions over a Chinese food lunch at PF Changs that changed my life.

Question #1, what was my exit strategy for my San Diego advertising and PR agency?

"Well Gary, after I run my firm for ten more years I am turning it over to someone and then I will teach consultants and coaches how to attract clients," I said. "My wife and I are going to retire to a college town and spend our life surrounded by trees and water."

His second question was, "How would you do that?" Excitedly I told him I would write books, make speeches, put on conferences, and teach at a university. There are so many consultants and coaches that are great at what they do, but no one has ever taught them the science of attracting clients.

Question #3: "You sound very passionate. Why are you waiting for ten years to follow your passion?"

That question stumped me because my thoughts were on my obligations, clients, and employees. I described them as "the wolf at my door." In truth, it was my own fear of failure.

The fourth question helped me process: "How could you get started right now in a small way?"

"I can send invitations for a free monthly lunch seminar in my office," I ventured. "The sandwiches would be on me and I'd share with consultants and coaches the science of finding clients."

My first free lunch seminar was the next month. The invitations were in the mail when the terrorist attack of September 11, 2001 took place in New York and Washington, DC. To my surprise, consultants and coaches actually showed up for my lunch seminars. After I explained my theories, the attendees asked how much I'd charge to be their coach. Soon they asked me to write books for them and teach them to give speeches that attract clients. Meanwhile, while five of the top ten advertising and PR firms in San Diego went out of business, my work helping consultants and coaches attract clients literally took over my business.

We renamed our company the New Client Marketing Institute. Over the next eight years I invested $2 million in scientifically researching how to attract high-paying clients. We even tied in with the Harvard Business School. My research revealed a proven way for consultants and coaches to obtain a marketing return on investment of 400 percent to 2000 percent. Along the way, I edited or was the ghostwriter on more than 150 business books.

Now I annually speak to thousands of consultants and coaches, teaching them writing and speaking strategies to attract high-paying clients and how to persuade with a story. In addition to running the New Client Marketing Institute and the Marketing With a Book and Speech Summits, in 2007 I accepted an appointment as a member of the marketing faculty and assistant dean for continuing education at the University of California, San Diego, a campus located in a grove of trees overlooking the Pacific Ocean.

In 2014 my quest took a new turn. I launched Indie Books International. Independent consultants, coaches, and business owners turn to us for help with the preparation, publication, and promotion of a book that grows their business, puts money in the bank, and helps them make the difference they want to make. Indie Books International was founded by two best-selling authors, Mark

LeBlanc and myself, who educate consultants and coaches that the publication of the book is the starting line, not the finish line.

I share my story in order to spread a message of encouragement to consultants and coaches who are good at what they do and need to learn the science of attracting high-paying clients.

This story isn't really about me, it is about you. Let me end with four questions for you.

1.  What is your marketing with a book and speech strategy?

2.  How would you do it?

3.  What are you waiting for?

4.  How could you get started in a small way?

My hope for you is success. If I can be of assistance, please let me know.

# APPENDIX A
## About
# THE AUTHOR

**H**enry DeVries, MBA is an expert on typing and talking: how consultants and coaches can maximize revenues by writing books and giving speeches. He is the co-founder and CEO of Indie Books International and has served as an editor, ghostwriter, or credited co-author of more than 150 business books. He is also a professional speaker on the topic of "Persuading With a Story," and teaches marketing and is the former assistant dean for continuing education at the University of California, San Diego. The founder of the New Client Marketing Institute, he speaks to thousands of consultants and coaches each year, teaching them successful tactics that bring them new clients. Along with his books — *Self-Marketing Secrets, Client Seduction, Pain Killer Marketing, Closing America's Job Gap*, and *How to Close a Deal Like Warren Buffett* — the buzz building tools of Henry DeVries have been used to dramatically increase revenues and leverage marketing budgets for two decades. In addition to authoring his own books, he ghostwrites at least four books a year. In his writing, speaking, and mentoring he reveals more than 1,000 pragmatic strategies to achieve marketing returns of 400 percent to 2000 percent. On a personal note, his goal is to visit every Major League Baseball ballpark, and has so far visited thirty-eight and has seven to go. Henry can be reached at henry@indiebooksintl.com or at 619-540-3031.

# APPENDIX B
# Sample Book
# PROPOSAL

**N**ote from Author: This is the book proposal Tom Searcy and I used to sell the book *How to Close a Deal Like Warren Buffett* to McGraw-Hill. The senior editor at McGraw-Hill said it was the best proposal she had seen in ten years because of the marketing plan.

## Cover Letter

Dear name

> *"Rule No. 1: Never lose money.*
> *Rule No. 2: Never forget rule No. 1."*
> — **Warren Buffett**

If you want to know how to close a deal, nobody does it better than Buffett.

There are many successful books available on Warren Buffett as an investor, and an equal amount on negotiating a deal. But *How to Close a Deal Like Warren Buffett* is the first book that analyzes the moves Buffett makes when closing deals and lets readers find out how they can do it too.

For those 45 million dealmakers in America on a quest to improve, *How to Close A Deal Like Warren Buffett* offers a special kind of wisdom. This book deconstructs the Buffett blueprint for deal making and gives readers a wealth of Warren wisdom.

My co-author, author and marketing educator Henry DeVries, and I are ready to deliver a 50,000-word manuscript in 90 days once we agree to terms. I have enclosed a brief synopsis and would be pleased to discuss your ideas for the manuscript.

> Sincerely,
>
> Tom Searcy
> Hunt Big Sales
> 10150 Lantern Road, Ste 110
> Fishers, IN 46037
> Phone: 317.816.4327
> Mobile: xxx-xxx-xxxx
> Email: tom@huntbigsales.com

# HOW TO CLOSE A DEAL LIKE WARREN BUFFETT

## BOOK SYNOPSIS

*By Tom Searcy and Henry DeVries*

### BOOK'S UNIQUE POSITIONING

If you want to know how to close a deal, nobody does it better than Buffett.

Why? The man knows how to talk about money when he's making deals. Warren Buffett is famous for doing mega-money deals with as little information as a few pages of business plans and the standard financials a company would submit to a bank to qualify for a loan.

What Buffett has when he goes into any deal discussion is an encyclopedic knowledge of how businesses work financially. He knows "their money," "their wallet," and how investments and outcomes should work. Follow his lead and you will close more business.

There are many books available on Warren Buffett as an investor and an equal amount on negotiating a deal. But *How to Close A Deal Like Warren Buffett* is the first book that analyzes the moves Buffett makes when closing deals and lets readers find out how they can do it too.

Consider this surprising statistic: There are 45 million people in America that make a living closing deals. That's more dealmakers than the population of Florida, Illinois, and Ohio combined.

For those dealmakers on a quest to improve, *How to Close A Deal Like Warren Buffett* offers a special kind of wisdom. This book deconstructs the Buffett blueprint for deal making and gives readers a wealth of Warren wisdom. Here are some examples strategically placed throughout the book:

**Warren Wisdom #27: You can't make a good deal with a bad person.** Every deal Buffett makes is sealed with a handshake. Then the lawyers come in and memorialize the details. If you are closing a deal with a bad person, there is no contract in the world that will protect you.

**Warren Wisdom #93: Complex calculations are not necessary.** "If calculus or algebra were required to be a great investor, I'd have to go back to delivering newspapers," admits Buffett. His uncommon gift for closing a deal is common sense. Simple mathematics and a logical brain is what you need to withstand the emotions of deal making, because emotions can get in the way of closing a deal.

**Warren Wisdom #19: Deal making is no-called strike game. Buffett says,** "You don't have to swing at everything — you can wait for your pitch." Buffett is fond of baseball and often uses the game to illustrate his philosophy. In deal making you get to stand at the plate all day, and you never have to swing. Sometimes the best deals are the ones you don't make.

## MARKET NEED FOR THIS BOOK

**Warren Wisdom #87: "You do things when the opportunities come along."** *Warren Buffett.*

This is a time of rapid changes in the marketplace, and also of great opportunities for those willing to follow Buffett's lead. There are three reasons the 45 million Americans who survive by making deals need this book:

1. The marketplace is polarizing into two ends of the spectrum: commodity transactions where you compete on price, and specialized offerings where you compete on differentiation. Too many are allowing themselves to be perceived as simple commodities in the eyes of the market or consumers.

2. Due to innovations on many fronts, the hybrid deals in the middle are vanishing. The middle road is really a no man's land where deals go to die.

3. The choice is clear. Either get really good at commoditized transactional deals and fight over market share, or grab market share by differentiating so you can close really big deals. This book teaches the reader the Warren Buffett way of how to do just that.

When it comes to deal making in the 21st century economy, you need to go big or go home. Premium positioning is the clear choice this book advocates. **Warren Wisdom #43:** "Your premium brand had better be delivering something special," warns Buffett, "or it's not going to get the business."

If you want to land the business, then you should go the biggest dealmaker in the world — Warren Buffett — to learn how.

## INTENDED AUDIENCE: THE CUSTOMERS FOR THIS BOOK

**Warren Wisdom #1:** "Money will always flow toward opportunity, and there is an abundance of that in America," Warren Buffett told his stockholders in 2011.

The targeted readers for this book are the 45 million business owners, entrepreneurs, sales professionals, and those in related occupations whose businesses live and die by getting money to flow toward the opportunities they represent. According to the 2010 U.S. Census, these include:

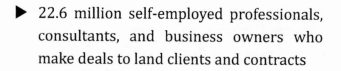

▶ 22.6 million self-employed professionals, consultants, and business owners who make deals to land clients and contracts

▶ 15.4 million sales professionals and related occupations (advertising sales, business development, insurance agents, real estate brokers and agents, sales reps, securities, and financial services)

▶ 5.8 million corporate CEOs, the chief dealmakers of their organizations

▶ 1 million business transaction attorneys who close deals on behalf of clients and for themselves

Other readers are equally interested in money flow and deal-making opportunities. Additionally this book will appeal to the millions of executives involved in corporate strategic planning (source: 2010 U.S. Census), the 565,000 entrepreneurs who create new businesses every month in America (source: Ewing Marion Kauffman Foundation) and the tens of thousands of people in the U.S.

employed in venture capital firms, investment banks, business brokers, and other facets of the mergers and acquisition industry (source: U.S. Bureau of Labor Statistics).

## ABOUT THE AUTHORS

**Tom Searcy** is a nationally recognized author, speaker, and the foremost expert in large account sales. By the age of 40, Searcy had led four corporations, transforming annual revenues of less than $15 million to as much as $200 million in each case. Since then, Searcy has launched Hunt Big Sales, a fast-growth consultancy and thought leadership organization. He's helped clients land more than $5 billion in new sales with 190 of the Fortune 500 companies, including 3M, Disney, Chase Bank, International Paper, AT&T, Apple and hundreds more. Tom is the author of *RFPs Suck! How to Master the RFP System Once and for All to Win Big Business* and the co-author of *Whale Hunting: How to Land Big Sales and Transform Your Company.*

**Henry J. DeVries** is an educator and author who speaks to thousands of business owners and executives each year, teaching them how to grow their businesses and advance their careers. As assistant dean, he has helped the continuing education arm of the University of California, San Diego grow enrollments in certificate programs 59 percent in four years. A former advertising and public relations agency president, he helped the firm double revenues and earn a spot in the Ad Age 500 by closing deals with clients like Petco, Marriott, and Sunkist. He is a weekly columnist for a daily business newspaper and a contributing editor to a quarterly careers magazine. Henry is the co-author of *Self-Marketing Secrets*, *Pain Killer Marketing*, and *Closing America's Job Gap*. He earned his MBA at San Diego State University and has completed management and leadership certificate programs at the Harvard Business School.

# MARKETING PLATFORM AND PLAN

## TOM SEARCY PROMOTION OPPORTUNITIES

As co-author and founder of Hunt Big Sales, Tom is committed to an intensive marketing campaign for this book. Tom connects actively and regularly with large audiences of prospective buyers, as a speaker, consultant, blogger, and web discussion host. He has a fully developed marketing plan that we have begun to launch. The overview of our plan is outlined in the chart on the following page.

### Speaking Engagements

Tom Searcy is a regular presenter for corporate markets and makes public appearances in venues focused on sales, marketing, and business development. Tom is a certified "expert speaker" for Vistage International, the largest network of CEOs in the world, counting 15,000 members in 15 countries. Tom earns rave reviews for these presentations, and is ranked in the top 1 percent of all Vistage presenters. In 2012 alone, Tom is already engaged for 30 CEO Vistage presentations throughout the country. These occasions are 4 hour workshops for 12-20 CEO's of companies between $2M and $500M in annual sales and an employee base of 10 – 500 employees.

In addition to Vistage, Tom receives many corporate speaking invitations, including the National Sporting Goods Association, Entertainment Corporate Marketing Solutions in 2011, and National Food Group in 2012, among others.

In every one of Tom's speaking engagements, he offers a response mechanism for attendees to give us their information and in turn receive free information from us, which contributes to the overall marketing campaign for this book.

## Tom Searcy's Engagement in the Online Community

Tom is a highly influential voice in the online community. He is a weekly, paid blogger for CBS's *MoneyWatch*, as the foremost expert in large account sales, with a distinct monthly readership of 3 million. He is also a paid, daily blogger for Inc. Magazine online, with a distinct monthly readership of 13 million, the majority of which are small to mid-sized business owners. He is a bi-weekly blog contributor and sales leadership expert for the Vistage online community. This community includes more than 15,000 companies, supporting a database of more than 1.8 million employees.

Tom also influences his followers through a robust database and nurture campaign of over 7,000 people, the majority of which have been contacts made through Tom's personal connection at various speaking engagements and corporate venues. On LinkedIn, he engages with his 4,000 contacts in discussions in the six highly active LinkedIn groups that he owns and administers. His following also includes a monthly open Q&A session called "Time with Tom" where CEOs and Presidents are invited to get feedback on their biggest sales challenges. Tom is also a sponsored webinar presenter for companies such as Citrix Online, Hoovers, Society for Marketing Professionals

Services, and Vistage International. He is also a webinar host, through strategic affiliate relationships, for companies such as VIPOrbit, Venturist, and Broadlook Technologies. In 2012 alone, he is scheduled to present or host twelve webinars, each of which will include promotional opportunities for this book.

All of these venues — Tom's blogs, LinkedIn connections, database of followers, webinar attendees, and affiliate companies, engage the target audience for this book and serve as excellent venues for endorsement. Tom is also already well positioned to market the book to the online community and owns the web domain "www.CloseDealsLikeBuffett.com."

**Weekly Tips**

Our "Weekly Tips" (a brief e-mail with a sales tip from Tom) are well received, well read, and forwarded, with an estimated readership of 10,000. Through our public speaking, we are able to add fresh subscribers each week. These subscribers are predominately Presidents and CEOs who are thought-leaders and have a strong tendency to recommend books and materials to peers and subordinates. In addition, they buy in bulk those books that they feel will most dramatically impact their staff.

## Prospective Endorsements

Through Tom's interview series called "5 Answers in 5 Minutes," Tom has developed relationships with the following sponsors who will promote, write a foreword or endorse on the back and in the inner covers, his book.

a.  Harvey MacKay – author of 2 *New York Times* bestsellers

b.  Jill Konrath – author of *Snap Selling and Selling to Big Companies*

c.  Jeffrey Gitomer – author of 12 *New York Times* bestsellers on sales

d.  Keith Ferrazzi – author of #1 *New York Times* Bestseller Who's Got Your Back

e.  Marshall Goldsmith – author of *New York Times* bestseller and *Wall Street Journal* top ten bestseller *MOJO – How to Get It, How to Keep It*, and *How to Get It Back When You Lose It!*

f.   Oren Klaff – author of *Pitch Anything*

g.   Daniel Waldschmidt – CEO at Waldschmidt ARP

As Tom adds other world-renowned experts to his interview series, this list will continue to grow.

## National Media Plan

As a regular columnist for CBS's *MoneyWatch*, Inc.com, and contributor to the *UK Financial Times* and *The Wall Street Journal*, Tom has active media contacts with editors and publishers that we intend to leverage in this marketing campaign. We will also be employing a national publicist, Bruce Serbin, who has been the hired publicist for over 25 authors who have achieved *New York Times* bestseller list status. We will be also be utilizing Tina LaSasso for direct sponsorship and network marketing campaign for book sales. Tina has worked with over 20 best-selling authors on launching their book promotion campaigns.

**Marketing Timetable**

**Strategies**

**Now 6-3 months pre-publication**

**3-0 months pre-publication**

**Post publication**

**Evangelists**

7,000 weekly tip readers + access to 16 million readers online

Vistage speeches to 30 CEO groups in 2011

Estimated 10,000 Vistage speeches to 30 CEO groups in 2012

Keynote speaking

Hosting 12 webinars in 2012

Estimated 13,000 Pre-publication reviews are circulated

Estimated 15,000 Reviews and recommendations are circulated

**Public Relations**

4,000   LinkedIn   connections,   6   active

groups

Seek endorsements

Interviews

Articles

Media connections

**Marketing Sponsors**

Harvey MacKay, Jill Konrath, Geoffrey Gitomer, Keith Ferrazzi, Marshall Goldsmith, Oren Klaff, Daniel Waldschmidt

Each sponsor gives notice of upcoming publication

Free first chapter offered to readers of sponsors

Reviews and recommendations published

**Sales**

National Publicist – Bruce Serbin

Book Marketing –Tina LaSasso

On-line tools created to enhance book

Supporting materials for book

Books purchased for each Vistage Presentation (estimated 25/presentation and 30 CEO presentations/year)

Book purchased for Keynote Speeches

(average – 150 books/keynote, anticipated 12-25 keynotes in 2012)

Books purchased for Training Programs – 25 book/program, at 12 programs scheduled for 2012

## HENRY DEVRIES PROMOTION OPPORTUNITIES

Henry writes a weekly column for the *San Diego Union-Tribune*, a metro daily newspaper with a circulation of 300,000.

Henry is a contributing editor for UC San Diego's *Prospectus* magazine, which has a circulation of 47,000 Southern California college graduates.

The book will also be promoted through the UC San Diego Extension opt-in e-mail list of 56,000 college graduates interested in career advancement.

Henry is the past president of the UC San Diego alumni association and will be able to obtain a feature in the alumni magazine, @

UCSD, which has a circulation of 113,000.

In addition to teaching marketing at UC San Diego, in the past year Henry spoke in San Diego, Seattle, Toronto, Minneapolis, and throughout the Los Angeles metro area. In the coming year Henry will speak in San Diego, New York, New Orleans, Minneapolis, and the Los Angeles metro area.

Henry speaks every month to business groups and business and continuing education schools (e.g. Columbia University, Clemson University, San Diego State University, California State University Northridge). Here are some potential tailored speech topics and audiences to offer talks based on the book:

▶ Closing Deals Like Warren Buffett for Advertising Agencies (Ad Clubs)

▶ Closing Deals Like Warren Buffett for Consultants (Institute of Management Consultants)

▶ Closing Deals Like Warren Buffett for Attorneys (Bar Associations)

▶ Closing Deals Like Warren Buffett for Sales Reps (In-House Corporate Groups, Sandler Sales Institutes)

▶ Closing Deals Like Warren Buffett for Financial Planners (Association of Professional Consultants, Women in Financial Planning)

▶ Closing Deals Like Warren Buffett for Entrepreneurs (Venture Capital Groups, Chamber of Commerce)

▶ Closing Deals Like Warren Buffett for Small Businesses (Chamber of Commerce, National Association of Business Women)

Henry is the founder of the New Client Marketing Institute, a training company that teaches professionals and consultants how to attract more clients. Henry blogs weekly on www.newclientmarketing.com. There are 2,500 subscribers to the New Client Marketing monthly e-Zine. Henry has 725 connections on LinkedIn, 350 friends on Facebook, and 105 followers on Twitter. Henry has a background in freelance journalism and public relations and would produce news releases, opinion pieces, and articles excerpted from the book for trade journals, magazines, and business journals.

## Possible Contributors for Endorsements and Foreword

Tom can approach either Harvey MacKay or Brian Tracy for the foreword.

The forewords for Henry's last two books were by Ken Blanchard and Guy Kawasaki, who Henry could approach for endorsements for this book.

Tom and Henry can also approach executives from Qualcomm, Sempra Energy, Petco, and Roche Diagnostics, as well as Harvey MacKay, Jill Konrath, Geoffrey Gitomer, Oren Klaff and Marshall Goldsmith for endorsements.

## Proposed Specifications

**Type of Book:** Business/Marketing and Sales

**Word Count:** 50,000 words

**Art:** Authors will provide their own art

**Proposed Manuscript Completion Date:**
May 15, 2012

**Special Interior Features:** The authors intend to provide QR codes or resource links supplemental materials including a Closing the Deal punch list, road map quiz, audio files at website, capture name and address, continue the conversation

**Competitive Analysis**

**Warren Wisdom #101:** "In the business world, the rear view mirror is always clearer than the windshield." Many books have looked back on Buffett as an investor and on ways to close a deal. Both books on Warren Buffett and examinations of closing a deal have done quite well. No book to date has combined these two topics.

*Beyond Dealmaking: Five Steps to Negotiating Profitable Relationships* by Melanie Billings-Yun (Jossey Bass, 2010). Filled with real-life examples of negotiations that have gone right and wrong, this book shows the author's view of how fairness, honesty, empathy, flexibility, and mutual problem solving lead to sustainable success. Dr. Billings-Yun has spent the past twenty years assisting international businesses, NGOs and public agencies with negotiations. This book does not contain the negotiation strategies of the world's greatest dealmaker, Warren Buffett.

*The Art of Closing Any Deal* by James Pickens (Business Plus, 2003). This book could more accurately be titled "How to Ruthlessly Lie, Manipulate and Use Mind Games To Make a Sale." A no-holds-barred guide to getting your way - not just in closing a sale, but in everything you do. This exceedingly detailed, candidly written guide to mind control sold more than a million copies. He uses anecdotes sparingly, but weaves in plenty of examples. This book does not contain the deal making philosophies of Warren Buffett, the man engaged in 70 distinct business lines.

*The Essays of Warren Buffett: Lessons for Corporate America* by Lawrence Cunningham

(Carolina Academic Press, 2001). Experienced readers of Warren Buffett's letters to the shareholders of Berkshire Hathaway Inc. receive valuable information about how to conduct business. These essays distill in plain words Buffett's basic principles of sound business practices. The book is not organized around any central theme such as deal making.

*The Snowball: Warren Buffett and the Business of Life* by Alice Schroeder (Bantam Books, 2009). The book was a #1 *New York Times* bestseller and the most comprehensive look into Warren Buffett's life and philosophies that the world is likely to ever see. The book was produced through five years of interviews with Buffett. The book covers every facet of his life, but is not organized around topics. The book contains no section on closing deals.

*The Tao of Warren Buffett* by Mary Buffett and David Clark (Scribner, 2006). Like the sayings of the ancient Chinese philospher Lao-tzu, Warren Buffett's worldly wisdom is deceptively simple and enormously powerful in application. These are the smart, funny, and memorable sayings that reveal the life philosophy and the investment strategies that have made Warren Buffett, and the shareholders of Berkshire Hathaway, so enormously wealthy. This book covers a broad spectrum and does not focus on the Warren Buffett approach to closing a deal.

*The Warren Buffet Way* by Robert G. Hagstrom (John Wiley & Sons, 2005). Originally published in 1994, the book has sold 1.2 million copies. Mostly about investing, the book does contain chapters on buying a business and the psychology of money. The book does not look at deal making.

*Thoughts of Chairman Buffet* compiled by Simon Reynolds (Harper Collins, 1998). This book is a collection of quotations gathered from a variety of sources. Warren Buffett did not participate or endorse the book. A small book of pithy sayings. Not an advice book on any topic, including closing a deal.

*Warren Buffett Speaks* by Janet Lowe (John Wiley & Sons, 2007). A second edition updated to reflect Warren Buffett's life in the previous 10 years; the book contains a collection of quotes, writing and favorite sayings from the world's most successful investor. Warren Buffett cooperated with the book project, as did his buddy Bill Gates. The quotes are well organized, but there is no section on deal making.

*Warren Buffett's Management Secrets* by Mary Buffett and David Clark (Simon & Schuster 2009). An in-depth look at Warren Buffett's philosophies for personal and professional management. Mary Buffett, Warren Buffett's ex daughter-in-law, gained her insights being married to Warren's son Peter for 12 years. The chapters cover topics like picking a company to work for, delegating, motivating employees and managerial challenges — nothing on deal making.

## OUTLINE OF CONTENTS

### Chapter 1: The Deal Making Blueprint of Warren Buffett

Warren Buffett might be catching a lot of flack these days, but if you want to know about closing big deals, he's still the guy to watch. Why? The man knows how to talk about money when he's deal making. What he has when he goes into any conversation is an encyclopedic knowledge of how businesses work financially. He knows "their money," "their wallet," and how investments and outcomes should work. Follow his lead and you will close more business.

## Chapter 2: Know the Other Guy's Money

How they make it, how they count it, how they spend it. This is obviously much easier to do for publicly traded companies. For privately held companies, the numbers are fairly easy to estimate — at least the cost of goods sold and probably the cost of sale. These numbers are critical to discussing the possibilities of working together. Too often the discussion stops at budget. When you don't know, ask. Not the trade secrets, but at least the industry averages. This provides a basic framework for the discussion.

## Chapter 3: Know the Other Guy's Wallet

How does this sale impact any of these critical

numbers? The terms of the deal should be looked at from their side of the table first, then yours. "When you hit your choking point, you quit," says Buffett. "I've walked away from deals before and meant it. I walked away from the See's (Candies) deal. They wanted $30 million, and we offered $25 million. We walked away and, fortunately for us, they walked after us," he said.

**Chapter 4: Start Discussing the Money Early**
You know you are going to discuss the money later. Early in the conversation, you do not have enough information for precision. Instead, you have an understanding of the economics of the prospect's industry, so you have enough to determine if a deal makes any sense at all. Use that economic information and industry knowledge to frame a shared understanding of the reality of the money for this opportunity. Warren Wisdom #23: "Never count on making a good sale," says Buffett. "Have the purchase price be so attractive that even a mediocre sale gives good results."

## Chapter 5: Use Ranges to Qualify and Disqualify

Understand early (and throughout the discussion) whether you and your prospect are in the same arena. By using ranges of prices, cost structures, yields, and performance you can both be sure that you are dealing in a shared reality rather than getting to the end and finding yourselves so far apart that there is permanent damage done to the relationship.

## Chapter 6: Speak the Language of Investment and Outcomes

Every large sale is an investment on both parts in an outcome. When you move the conversation from price to investment and cost to outcomes you are focusing on the business impact rather than budget impact. This is the language of large sales. Here is an eyewitness account of a deal that unraveled recently because the players did not observe these guidelines. The sale involved the installation of a point-of-sale system into a retail chain. The details are complicated as many large deals are, but the numbers were simple:

If you calculated the investment necessary for the system, the transaction cost was going to be >5 percent of the transaction revenue value. That's more than the cost of the charge card processing fee! Never going to work regardless of the reporting bells and whistles, speed to data consolidation and so on. This violates the entire Buffett blueprint. The selling team did not understand the fundamental money issues of their prospect. They had not asked, done their research or even estimated. They were focused on the features of their system and what they had heard the IT people say would be the selection criteria without working through the money issues. That always leads to disaster.

## Chapter 7: Don't Discount Early

You regularly hear fearful "dealmakers" use language like, "Let's not let money get in the way of working together." There's a word for this that is not used in polite company. This is the language of discounting before the scope has been clearly defined. The sales person believes that he is being clever by taking money off the table. What he has really done

is to take margin off the table, his and his company's margin. If qualifying investment and impact has been made up front, then this point does not need to be made again.

### Chapter 8: Don't Negotiate Until it's Time

Work on the deal points one at a time. Work through the investment and outcome ideas clearly, then negotiate. True, all of these points require negotiation. However, too often the conversation turns to negotiations too early before real scope and deliverables have been defined. Which means that the whole is reduced to the little parts before the shared picture of the whole has been established.

### Chapter 9: Biggest Deal Making Blunders (and How to Avoid them Buffett Style)

Warren Buffett's savvy deal making abilities coupled with his pleasing personality allowed him to achieve business success like no other. But even the wealthiest man in the world makes an error or two. Warren Wisdom #33: "Rule No. 1: Never lose money. Rule No. 2: Never forget rule No. 1."

# APPENDIX

**101 Warren Wisdoms**

**Further Readings**

**About the Authors**